■ SCHOLASTIC

VOCABULARY-BUILDING
Card Games

GRADE 3

BY LIANE B. ONISH

NEW YORK • TORONTO • LONDON • AUCKLAND • SYDNEY
MEXICO CITY • NEW DELHI • HONG KONG • BUENOS AIRES

Teaching Resources

Hi, Mom!

Editor: Joan Novelli
Cover design by Maria Lilja.
Interior design by Kathy Massaro.
Interior art by Anne Kennedy.

ISBN 13: 978-0-439-55466-4
ISBN 10: 0-439-55466-7

Copyright © 2008 by Liane B. Onish.
Published by Scholastic Inc.
All rights reserved.
Printed in the U.S.A.

2 3 4 5 6 7 8 9 10   40   14 13 12 11 10

Contents

Game	Skill Focus	Page
Wordy Concentration	Word Meaning	12
Orderly Races	Alphabetical Order	13
Vocabo!	Definitions	14
Synonym Slap-Down	Synonyms	16
Birds in a Tree	Word Meaning	18
Voc-Anagrams	Anagrams	21
Compound Charades	Word Structure	24
Vocabulary Password	Word Knowledge	27
Picture This!	Meaning Clues	28
As You Like It	Similes	30
Mail Call	Word Knowledge	33
Word Shark	Prefixes and Suffixes	34
Hidden Homophones	Easily Confused Words	38
Sentence-Ology	Words in Context	44
Voca-Bees	Words in Context	46
Cloze Call	Context Clues	47
What's in a Word?	Word Features	49
Vocabulary Baseball	Vocabulary Word Recall	50
Sorting Hats	Parts of Speech	51
Opposites Attract	Antonyms	52

About This Book

Word Selection

The words in this book support vocabulary development for grade 3 as follows:

❋ One hundred words are high-frequency, nondecodable words, all essential to reading, writing, and comprehension.

❋ Other words have been chosen from grade-level literature and will be key additions to students' growing vocabularies.

What the Research Says

"Intuition tells us that more practice leads to better memory. Research tells us something more precise: Memory in either the short- or long-term requires ongoing practice."

(Willingham, 2004)

Vocabulary games make words fun to learn and easier to remember, strengthening reading and literacy skills and much more. The more words children can recognize easily, the more they will read; and the more children read, the more words they will know, which will make them better and more willing readers and stronger speakers, spellers, writers, and test takers. This book offers a variety of fun games and activities designed to provide practice in recognizing, reading, and using more than 200 words, all key additions to students' growing vocabularies.

Research shows that vocabulary is correlated with student success. "Having a strong vocabulary is of particular importance to students in that it contributes significantly to achievement both in the subjects of their school curriculum and also on standardized tests" (Shostak, 2002). Direct instruction and reading widely are both important factors in increasing students' vocabulary. Repeated exposure to words and independent practice with them are also essential, and word games are an effective way to provide these opportunities. The games in this book support both the playful approach and level of practice that students need, and can be played again and again to build and deepen word knowledge, strengthen related skills, and make the learning stick.

How Much Practice?

"How much practice is the right amount? . . . It is difficult to overstate the value of practice. For a new skill to become automatic or for new knowledge to become long-lasting, sustained practice, *beyond the point of mastery,* is necessary" (Willingham, 2004). Research shows that we need about 12 encounters with, or exposures to, a new word before we know it well enough to comprehend it in text (McKeown, Beck, Omanson, & Pople, 1985; as cited in Beck, McKeown, & Kucan, 2002). Enough encounters with a word and it will find its way into our oral and written vocabularies. Vocabulary games, as a regular part of classroom life, can give children the multiple encounters they need to "own" more words.

What's Inside?

In addition to 20 word games, you'll find extra game cards and blank game card templates for customizing games, and a master list of target words for easy reference and for fluency practice. Here's a closer look at each section of the book.

Pages 9–11: Master Word List

This game-by-game list of words is provided for easy reference. You can also use this list to create speed drill practice for reading fluency and automaticity. (For more information on this, see More Ways to Use the Word Cards, page 8.)

Pages 12–60: Vocabulary Games

Directions for 20 vocabulary-building games follow a simple format to make it easy for students to set up and play.

* **Skill:** All games are designed to build vocabulary. Some games may have additional areas of instructional focus, such as recognizing parts of speech.

* **Number of Players:** Games provide opportunities for varied groupings, from one or two students to the entire class.

* **Object of the Game:** How to win varies from game to game.

* **Materials:** In addition to game cards, this section lists any other materials students need to play, such as a timer, crayons, or index cards.

* **How to Play:** Step-by-step directions make it easy to set up and get started.

* **More Ways to Play:** Use the suggestions in this section to create simpler or more challenging games to meet the learning needs of different groups of students.

Each game focuses on a set of words. For some games, such as Orderly Races (page 13), you will select the game cards from other games or from the extra cards (pages 62–80), or use the blank game card templates (page 61) to create your own. For other games, such as As You Like It (page 30), target words are specified and game cards are provided accordingly. However, for any of the games, you can use the extra game cards and blank game card templates to customize vocabulary.

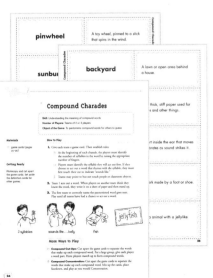

Teaching Tip

You'll find that many of the games work with cards from other games, as well as with the extra cards. You can also adapt the games for use with specific content area vocabulary. Simply copy the blank game card templates and fill in desired words. Review the game with those words in mind and make any adjustments that might be necessary.

Pages 61–80: Extra Game Cards

These pages feature extra game cards for use with specific games as well as for customizing any game. The Wild Cards (page 61) are for use with Wordy Concentration (page 12), but you may also find them useful to create variations on other games. The Bee Cards (page 61), used with Voca-Bees (page 46), can also serve as playful game card templates for any game in which you are creating word cards. Blank game card templates (page 61) are also provided for this purpose. In addition, there are 95 extra word cards (pages 62–80), useful for games that specify "any word cards," and to customize the word card set for other games. As with the words preselected for various games, these extra word cards support vocabulary development for high-frequency words, which supports fluency in reading.

Teaching With the Games

You can use the games in any order that best supports your teaching needs. The Contents page summarizes specific skills to assist with game selection.

Setup and Storage

Once you choose a game and gather any necessary materials, it's worth the effort to take a few minutes to set up a storage system. With the setup that follows, students can easily use the games at school as well as transport them home to play with families, reinforcing the connections between home and school that lead to more successful learning.

1. For durability, photocopy the game cards on cardstock, or glue them to index cards and laminate.

2. Clip the cards for each game together (or place them in an envelope) and store in a resealable plastic bag. Consider making a second set of cards for each game as backup. (Place these in an envelope and label "Extra Set of Cards.")

3. Label each bag with the name of the game, the skill it reinforces, and the number of players.

4. Photocopy the directions and tape them to the inside of the bag.

Introducing the Games

Introduce the games one at a time in any order that best matches your language arts program and your students' needs. Model how to play, including for individual players, pairs, small groups, and the whole class.

(See Number of Players for each game.) Keep in mind that the games provide support for differentiated learning. Each game includes suggestions for variations, including, for example, using fewer or more word cards and simplifying or increasing the level of vocabulary difficulty. You may also choose games to use with students based on an identified need. Students who need additional practice with easily confused words, for example, will benefit from playing Hidden Homophones (page 38). Word Shark (page 34) is just right for students who need practice recognizing prefixes and suffixes and understanding how they affect word meaning.

Who Goes First?

There are many ways to decide who goes first in a game. Here are a few ideas students can choose from.

❄ Use a single die. Have players roll the die. The player who rolls the highest number goes first. The next player is the one sitting clockwise from the first player. For variety, have the player who rolls the lowest number go first.

❄ Use the first initial of each player's name. The player whose name is closest to *A* (or *Z*) goes first, with the other players following clockwise.

❄ Mix up the word cards for the game. Deal one card to each player. The player whose word is closest to *A* (or *Z*) goes first.

More Ways to Use the Word Cards

In addition to using the word cards to play the games in this book, there are many other ways you can use them to provide the practice students need to achieve long-lasting learning. Following are some suggestions.

❄ **My Words!** Give students a bag or box to use for their personal game cards and other vocabulary words. Periodically, have them select a random handful to use in games, such as Wordy Concentration (page 12), Orderly Races (page 13), Vocabulary Password (page 27), Mail Call (page 33), Sentence-Ology (page 44), and Vocabulary Baseball (page 50), as well as in their story writing.

❄ **Curriculum Vocabulary:** Use the blank game card templates (page 61) to create content area word cards. Fill in the word, leaving the definition space blank. Have students complete the cards by writing the definitions, using their textbooks or dictionaries as a resource. Then have them write sentences on the reverse side.

Teaching Tip

As students revisit games and words, encourage them to use prior knowledge to make new connections. Is there a synonym, antonym, or homonym they know? Can they give a definition or use the word in context? When they come to an unknown word, do they recognize part of the word from another word they know? How can they use what they know to make sense of an unfamiliar word?

Bibliography

Beck, I. L., McKeown, M. G., & Kucan, L. (2002). *Bringing Words to Life: Robust Vocabulary Instruction.* New York: The Guilford Press.

Blevins, W. (2006). *Phonics From A to Z: A Practical Guide* (2nd ed.). New York: Scholastic.

Fry, E. B., & Kress, J. E. (2006). *The Reading Teacher's Book of Lists* (5th ed.). San Francisco, CA: Jossey-Bass.

Kamil, M. L., Mosenthal, P. B., Pearson, P. D., & Barr, R. (Eds.). (2000). *Handbook of Reading Research, Vol. III.* Mahwah, NJ: Lawrence Erlbaum Associates.

Shostak, J. (2002). "The Value of Direct and Systematic Vocabulary Instruction." Retrieved September 27, 2007, from www.sadlier-oxford.com/docs/pdf/9147-9_VW_WhitePaper_Vol7.pdf.

Willingham, D. T. (2004, Spring). "Practice Makes Perfect—But Only if You Practice Beyond the Point of Perfection." *American Educator.*

❈ **Matching Activities:** Make a class set of all the word cards and a set of all the definition cards. Keep them in separate boxes or large baskets. Use them by the handful (presorting to match word and definition cards) in matching activities. For example, students can match words to their definitions, or match words to synonyms or antonyms.

❈ **Card Collectors:** Give students several blank game card templates to use as bookmarks for their independent reading. Let them choose a word from their daily reading to share with a book group. Have them write the word in the space provided on the left and add a definition in the space on the right. They can also quote the sentence from the book, or use the word in a sentence of their own, on the reverse side.

❈ **Fluency Practice:** Use the word cards as a resource for fluency practice. Select a handful of cards at random. Let children practice reading the words until they are ready to be timed.

A Note About Word Parts

Learning to break longer words into smaller, recognizable parts is an essential tool for vocabulary development. Of new words a student encounters in reading, approximately 60 percent can be analyzed into parts that provide significant help in determining meaning (Nagy & Anderson, 1984; as cited in Kamil, Mosenthal, Pearson, & Barr, 2000). A study of Greek and Latin roots helps students build knowledge of word parts. Greek and Latin were influential languages, and they contributed roots for many everyday words to other languages. For example, the Greek word *teckhne* means "something made by human intelligence," and it forms the root of our words *technical* and *technique.*

You can build students' base for comprehension by looking for opportunities as they play the games in this book to point out and teach common Greek and Latin roots. For example, students playing As You Like It (page 30) can learn about the Latin root *delicate* (Latin: *delicatus* meaning "pleasing") and use this knowledge to figure out the meaning of other words they encounter, such as *delicatessen, delicious,* and *delicacy.*

Master Word List

Wordy Concentration (page 12)

Any ten words from other games or from the extra game cards (pages 62–80).

Orderly Races (page 13)

Any ten or more words from other games or from the extra game cards (pages 62–80).

Vocabo! (page 14)

Any words (at least 24) from other games or from the extra game cards (pages 62–80).

Synonym Slap-Down (page 16)

aid	join
angry	just
assist	link
attach	mad
barely	noise
connect	only
din	racket
furious	support
hardly	uproar
help	upset

Birds in a Tree (page 18)

Any eight–ten words from other games or from the extra game cards (pages 62–80).

Voc-Anagrams (page 21)

inch/chin	salts/lasts
melon/lemon	snail/nails
ocean/canoe	study/dusty
pools/spool	ticks/stick
reef/free	waist/waits

Compound Charades (page 24)

backyard	starfish
cardboard	sunburn
eardrum	supermarket
footprint	teaspoon
pinwheel	watchdog

Vocabulary Password (page 27)

Any 20 words from other games or from the extra game cards (pages 62–80).

Picture This! (page 28)

escape	handsome
factory	library
freezing	

As You Like It (page 30)

beautiful	happy
clumsy	lost
delicate	smart
difficult	strange
frighten	strong

Mail Call (page 33)

Any words from other games or from the extra game cards (pages 62–80).

Word Shark (page 34)

Prefixes:	Roots:
re-	check
un-	clean
	cover
Suffixes:	do
-ed	fair
-er	fold
-est	kind
-ing	pack
-less	paint
-ly	view
-ness	
-s	

Hidden Homophones (page 38)

been	by	their	witch
bin	one	there	wood
blew	right	too	won
blue	sea	two	would
buy	see	which	write

Sentence-Ology (page 44)

Any 30 words from other games or from the extra game cards (pages 62–80).

Voca-Bees (page 46)

Any 10–20 words from other games or from the extra game cards (pages 62–80).

Cloze Call (page 47)

Groups of five or more words that fit a category. Sample categories/words provided for this game (substitute others as desired):

* **Prefixes:** discontinue, discount, displease, disrespect, distrust
* **Synonyms/Antonyms:** happy, healthy, loud, mild, smart
* **Words That Begin With *a*:** acrobat, approach, arrange, asleep, awful
* **Three-Syllable Words:** allergic, capital, dinosaur, interview, messenger
* **Size:** enormous, huge, mammoth, minute, towering
* **Clothing:** goggles, kimono, shawl, suspenders, vest
* **Geography:** canyon, island, peninsula, stream, valley
* **Proper Nouns:** Abraham Lincoln, Caribbean Sea, Grand Canyon, Hawaii, Statue of Liberty
* **Sports:** dribble, field, goal, slide, steal
* **Sensory Descriptions:** fragile, juicy, scratchy, soothing, spicy

What's in a Word? (page 49)

Any multisyllabic words from other games or from the extra game cards (pages 62–80).

Vocabulary Baseball (page 50)

Any words from other games or from the extra game cards (pages 62–80).

Sorting Hats (page 51)

Any nouns, verbs, adjectives, and adverbs from other games or from the extra game cards (pages 62–80).

Opposites Attract (page 52)

above	break	front	question
add	cry	get	repair
all	different	give	same
answer	dislike	hear	shout
asleep	earn	heavy	spend
awake	end	ignore	subtract
back	enjoy	laugh	tame
begin	evening	light	true
below	false	morning	whisper
blame	forgive	none	wild

Extra Game Cards (page 62)

absent	found	round
adventure	full	seize
again	going	shall
always	group	should
around	grow	simply
astronaut	held	sometimes
away	idea	start
because	its	straight
behind	it's	sure
believe	just	talk
bring	knew	target
call	learn	these
carry	left	those
city	live	though
complete	may	thought
could	measure	through
curtain	middle	together
daughter	monitor	trouble
does	monster	upon
done	month	usual
draw	much	vacant
during	music	village
easily	must	walk
either	neither	warm
enough	never	while
example	once	word
fantasy	plenty	worth
far	problem	year
flavor	pull	yesterday
fly	put	young
follow	ready	zone
fortune	remain	

Wordy Concentration

Skill: Matching words and definitions

Number of Players: 2 or more

Object of the Game: To collect the most word and definition sets

Materials

※ game cards (any)

※ blank game card templates (page 61; optional)

※ Wild Cards (page 61; optional)

Getting Ready

Photocopy and cut apart any 10 word and definition cards, such as those for Synonym Slap-Down (page 16), Compound Charades (page 24), and Picture This! (page 28), for a total of 20 cards. Or use the game card templates (page 61) to create your own set of word and definition cards. Include Wild Cards if desired.

How to Play

1. Shuffle all cards (words and definitions) and place them facedown in a 5 x 4 array.

2. Play as you would play Concentration. The first player turns over two cards. If the cards show a word and its definition, the player keeps the pair and turns over two more cards. If the two cards do not match, the player turns them facedown and the next player takes a turn. If using Wild Cards, players turning them over can use them for any word or definition as needed to make a match.

3. The winner is the player with the most pairs.

More Ways to Play

※ **Words + Blanks Concentration:** Add blank cards (page 61) to the deck. When a player turns over a blank card, the player may write a word or a definition on it as needed to make a match. You may allow players to use a dictionary to find definitions. If a player turns over two blank cards, the player may write any word and its definition on the cards to make a match.

※ **Mini-Maxi Wordy Concentration:** Use fewer or more word and definition cards.

※ **Synonym, Antonym, or Homophone Wordy Concentration:** Use synonym, antonym, or homophone cards in place of the definition cards.

Orderly Races

Skill: Alphabetizing

Number of Players: 1 or 2 players, or teams

Object of the Game: To arrange vocabulary words in alphabetical order

How to Play

One or Two Players:

1. Give an equal number of cards to each player.

2. Set the timer for three minutes.

3. The players arrange the cards in alphabetical order.

4. At the end of three minutes, the players count the number of cards in correct alphabetical order. The player with the most cards in the correct order wins.

Teams:

1. Place a set of cards facedown in front of each team. (Include at least one card for each player.) Designate a table or whiteboard tray as a playing field for each team.

2. The teams line up some distance from their playing field.

3. The first player takes the top card and runs to the team's playing field. The player places the card about where it should go in alphabetical order. For example, the word card *answer* should be placed on the far left of the playing field, the word card *yesterday* on the far right. The player runs to the back of the line.

4. Each player adds one card to the team's playing field, and rearranges the cards as needed.

5. The first team to accurately arrange their cards on the playing field in alphabetical order wins.

More Ways to Play

* **Reverse Order:** Play to arrange the cards in order from *Z* to *A*.

* **Look to the Fourth Letter:** For a challenge, choose cards that require players to alphabetize to the fourth letter (or second, first, or third, depending on level of ability).

Materials

* game cards (any)
* blank game card templates (page 61; optional)
* timer
* table or whiteboard tray (for teams)

Getting Ready

Photocopy and cut apart any set of ten or more word cards. (Set definition cards aside for other games.) Each player or team will need an equal number of cards, but not necessarily the same set of cards. Or use the blank game card templates (page 61) to customize game cards.

Teaching Tip

As a variation, do not use a timer. The first player to correctly alphabetize his or her cards wins.

Vocabo!

Skill: Identifying vocabulary words from definitions

Number of Players: Any

Object of the Game: To color five words in a row going down, across, or diagonally

Materials

* game board (page 15)
* game cards (any)
* light-colored crayons

Getting Ready

Photocopy a game board for each player. Photocopy and cut apart a selection of at least 24 word and definition cards from other games, such as Opposites Attract (page 52) or from the extra game cards (pages 62–80). Select more than 24 words to allow students choice in the words they write on their game boards.

How to Play

1. Shuffle the word cards and the definition cards and place them in two separate piles.

2. Take each word card in turn and read the word aloud. Players write each word in any space on their game boards. Set the word cards aside. If playing with more than 24 words, students may choose which words they want to write on their boards. In this case, let them know in advance how many words they can skip. For example, if you have 30 words, players may skip any 6 words.

3. Play as you would play Bingo. Select and read a definition card. Players look for the word on their game board that goes with the definition. Then players use their crayons to shade in the box.

4. Continue reading the definition cards in order until one player has five words in a row, horizontally, vertically, or diagonally, and calls, "Vocabo!"

More Ways to Play

* **Synonym or Antonym Vocabo!** Use synonyms or antonyms in place of definition cards.

* **What's the Word?** In advance, prepare game cards with definitions in the spaces, rather than words. Make assorted game boards (with definitions in different spots) so that players have different game boards. Read the word cards one at a time. Players shade the space on their game board with the matching definition.

Name _____

Date _____

Vocabo!

		Free! Gratis! Complimentary!		

Vocabulary-Building Card Games: Grade 3 © 2008 by Liane B. Onish, Scholastic Teaching Resources

Synonym Slap-Down

Skill: Identifying synonyms

Number of Players: 5

Object of the Game: To collect sets of synonym cards

Materials

❄ game cards (page 17)

❄ blank game card templates (page 61)

Getting Ready

Photocopy and cut apart the word cards. Set aside the definition cards for use with other games. Write the following 15 synonyms on the blank game cards (one word per card):

angry: mad, furious, upset

help: assist, aid, support

join: connect, link, attach

only: just, barely, hardly

noise: din, uproar, racket

Teaching Tip

Encourage use of a thesaurus in this game as students check the words in a winning hand to confirm that they are all synonyms. A thesaurus is a terrific teaching tool for developing a broader vocabulary, building an understanding of subtle differences among similar words, and enhancing writing skills.

How to Play

1. Shuffle the game cards and synonym cards together and deal four cards to each player. This is each player's slap-down deck.

2. Players keep their hand hidden from the other players and select a card they do not want, keeping in mind that they want to eventually collect four words that are synonyms—for example, *assist, aid, support, help.*

3. Each player places the unwanted card facedown on the table. When all players have placed a card in front of them, everyone slides their unwanted card to the player on their left.

4. Players pick up the card that was passed, and repeat step 3, again selecting an unwanted card, placing it on the table, and passing it to the player on the left.

5. Play continues in this way until one player has four matching synonym cards and slaps the hand on the table.

6. Other players check the winning hand to confirm that the four words are synonyms.

More Ways to Play

❄ **Add a Category:** To keep the game fresh (or add players), add categories. Use the blank game card templates to make four cards for each new category.

❄ **Synonym Sleuths:** Mix up the cards and give one card to each player. Tell players not to look at their cards until you say "Go." Say "Go," and have players find the classmates who have synonyms for their word.

angry

Wanting to argue or fight.

help

To assist.

join

To fasten two things together.

noise

A sound, usually a loud or unpleasant one.

only

Not more than.

Vocabulary-Building Card Games: Grade 3 © 2008 by Liane B. Onish, Scholastic Teaching Resources

Birds in a Tree

Skill: Matching words and definitions

Number of Players: Any number of individuals or pairs

Object of the Game: To match definitions on birds to words on leaves in the tree

Materials

❋ game board (page 19)

❋ game cards (page 20)

❋ timer (optional)

Getting Ready

Photocopy a game board for each player. Using other games (or the extra game cards, pages 62–80) as a resource, write a definition on each leaf cluster of the tree. You can create a different set of game boards (different definitions or the same definitions in different positions) or write the definitions on a master copy of the game board and then photocopy for each player. Photocopy and cut apart the bird cards. On each bird write a vocabulary word to go with each definition. You may also create several distracter cards with words that do not match definitions on the game board.

How to Play

1. Give each player a game board and a set of game (word) cards.

2. At the start of the timer, players begin to place the birds on their tree to match the definitions on the leaves.

3. Players stand up to show they are finished, having matched each bird with a leaf cluster. (Distracter birds/words will be left over.)

4. Check that players have correctly matched words and definitions.

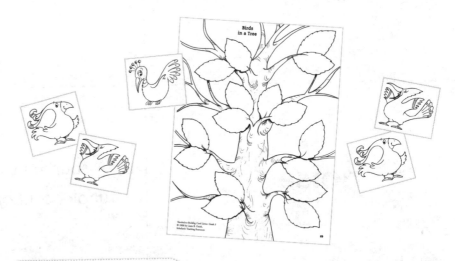

More Ways to Play

❋ **Time Out on a Limb:** Play until the whole class or group has completed the trees. Record the time. Play again later in the week and compare times.

❋ **Out on a Limb, Branch, or Arm:** Fill in the game board by writing a word in one of the leaves in each cluster. On game cards (birds), write synonyms or antonyms for each word. Have players place birds on the tree accordingly.

Birds
in a Tree

Birds in a Tree

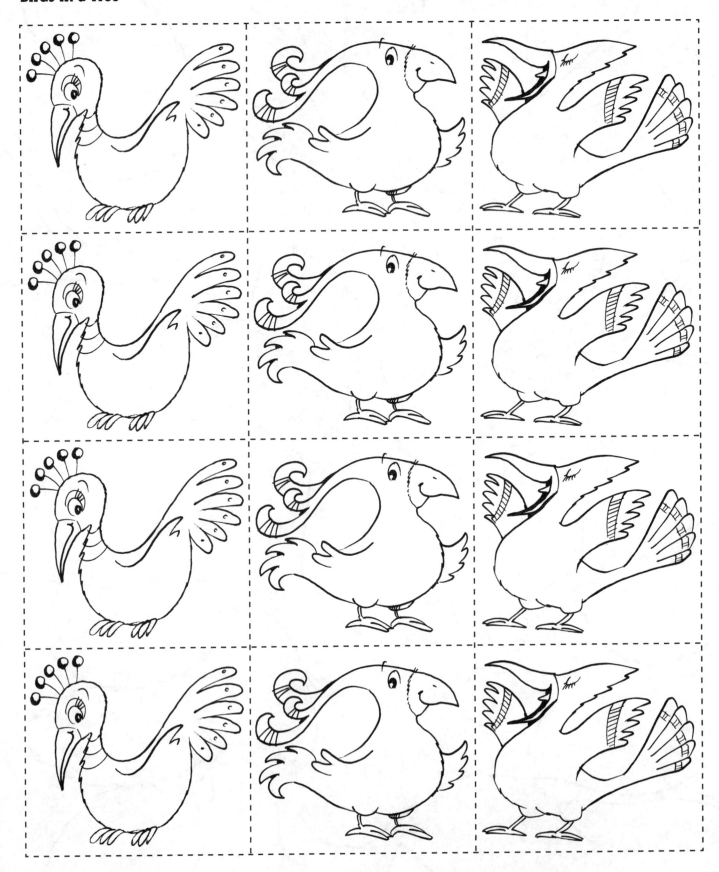

Voc-Anagrams

Skill: Using the same letter cards to spell two different words

Number of Players: 2 teams

Object of the Game: To arrange a set of letter cards to spell the answer to a clue, and then rearrange the same letters to spell the answer to a second clue

How to Play

1. Divide the class into two teams. Appoint team captains. Give each team a set of letter cards. Team captains distribute letters to players. Some players may have more than one letter.

2. Tell students that this game involves anagrams: words made by rearranging the letters of another word. You will begin by reading a clue. When a team figures out the answer to the clue, it is the captain's job to call out the letters needed, while players arrange themselves in that order to spell the answer. Teams will then receive a second clue, the answer to which can be spelled with the same letters. Captains rearrange the players to spell the new word.

3. Demonstrate by giving teams this clue: "A large animal related to a monkey but with no tail." Have team captains call out letters *a*, *p*, and *e*, as players arrange themselves in that order to spell the answer (*ape*). Then give a second clue: "A small, round green vegetable that grows as a seed in a pod." Captains rearrange the players to spell the answer (*pea*).

4. When all players understand how to play, begin the game. The first team to correctly spell the answer to the first clue gets 2 points. The first team to correctly spell the second word in a round gets 1 point.

5. The team that scores the most points wins.

More Ways to Play

❋ **Daily Anagram:** Post a daily pair of clues, along with scrambled letters for spelling the answers. Challenge students to figure out how to rearrange the letters before the end of the day to spell a new word. You might provide letter tiles at a nearby table to encourage a hands-on approach to this activity.

❋ **Anagram Authors:** Invite each team to write a set of clues to a new anagram. Have teams exchange clues and use their letters to spell the answers. (Use the blank letter cards as needed to add extra letters to the set.)

Materials

❋ game cards (pages 22–23)

❋ 2 envelopes

Getting Ready

Photocopy and cut apart the game cards (letters and clues). Make a set of letter cards for each team. Place each set in an envelope.

a	c	d	e
e	f	h	i
k	l	m	n
o	o	p	r
s	s	t	u
w	y		

Vocabulary-Building Card Games: Grade 3 © 2008 by Liane B. Onish, Scholastic Teaching Resources

Vocabulary-Building Card Games: Grade 3 © 2008 by Liane B. Onish, Scholastic Teaching Resources

Voc-Anagram Clues

1. A kind of worm or part of a ruler. (inch)

2. This is part of your face. (chin)

Voc-Anagram Clues

1. A large body of saltwater. (ocean)

2. A boat you move by paddling. (canoe)

Voc-Anagram Clues

1. Cantaloupe or honeydew is this kind of fruit. (melon)

2. This fruit is sour. (lemon)

Voc-Anagram Clues

1. Coral makes this place where many kinds of fish live. (reef)

2. Costs nothing. (free)

Voc-Anagram Clues

1. You can learn to swim in these places. (pools)

2. Thread comes on this. (spool)

Voc-Anagram Clues

1. These make food taste better. (salts)

2. A thing that keeps going _____. (lasts)

Voc-Anagram Clues

1. Fasten a belt around this part of your body. (waist)

2. If he hangs around, he _____ . (waits)

Voc-Anagram Clues

1. A clock does this again and again. (ticks)

2. Tape or glue will do this. (stick)

Voc-Anagram Clues

1. This animal moves very slowly. (snail)

2. Use a hammer to put these in. (nails)

Voc-Anagram Clues

1. Do this before a test. (study)

2. If something is this, it needs cleaning. (dusty)

Compound Charades

Skill: Understanding the meaning of compound words

Number of Players: Teams of 2 or 3 players

Object of the Game: To pantomime compound words for others to guess

Materials

❋ game cards (pages 25–26)

Getting Ready

Photocopy and cut apart the game cards. Set aside the definition cards for other games.

How to Play

1. Give each team a game card. Then establish rules:

   ❋ At the beginning of each charade, the players must identify the number of syllables in the word by raising the appropriate number of fingers.

   ❋ Players must identify the syllable they will act out first. If they choose to act out a word that rhymes with the syllable, they must first touch their ear to indicate "sounds like."

   ❋ Teams may point to but not touch people or classroom objects.

2. Team 1 acts out a word. When players on another team think they know the word, they write it on a sheet of paper and then stand up.

3. The first team to correctly name the pantomimed word goes next. Play until all teams have had a chance to act out a word.

3 syllables

sounds like … belly

fish

jellyfish

(More Ways to Play)

❋ **Compound Cut-Ups:** Cut apart the game cards to separate the words that make up each compound word. For a large group, give each player a word part. Have players match up to form compound words.

❋ **Compound Concentration:** Cut apart the game cards to separate the words that make up each compound word. Mix up the cards, place facedown, and play as you would Concentration.

backyard

A lawn or open area behind a house.

cardboard

Very thick, stiff paper used for boxes and other things.

eardrum

A part inside the ear that moves or vibrates as sound strikes it.

footprint

A mark made by a foot or shoe.

jellyfish

A sea animal with a jellylike body.

Vocabulary-Building Card Games: Grade 3 © 2008 by Liane B. Onish, Scholastic Teaching Resources

pinwheel | A toy wheel, pinned to a stick that spins in the wind.

sunburn | Sore, red skin caused by staying in sunlight too long.

supermarket | A large store that sells food and other items.

teaspoon | A small spoon used for stirring liquids or measuring.

watchdog | A dog trained to guard.

Vocabulary-Building Card Games: Grade 3 © 2008 by Liane B. Onish, Scholastic Teaching Resources

Vocabulary Password

Skill: Identifying vocabulary words from meaning clues

Number of Players: Pairs

Object of the Game: To name as many vocabulary words as possible in one minute

How to Play

Materials

- game cards (any)
- game card templates (page 61; optional)
- minute timer

1. Each pair of players mixes up the cards and divides them into two equal piles.

2. Play as you would play Password. Player 1 looks at the first word card without showing it to player 2. When player 1 is ready, start the timer. Player 1 gives clues without using the word. Player 2 tries to guess the word. When player 2 correctly identifies the word, he or she takes the card. Either player may say "Pass" to move on to the next word.

3. Play continues for 60 seconds.

4. Then players switch roles and use the second pile of word cards. The pair collaboratively scores 1 point for each word they correctly guess (totaling points from both rounds).

Getting Ready

Photocopy and cut apart any 20 word cards for each pair of players. Set aside any definition cards for other games. Or use the blank game card templates to create sets of word cards based on the week's vocabulary or areas of study.

More Ways to Play

- **Challenge Round:** Add word cards to each set that represent more sophisticated vocabulary. Use a different color for these words to highlight them for players as challenge words. Double the score for each of these words correctly identified.

- **Repeat Round:** Have players keep track of their scores and play again with the same partners and words. Challenge players to increase their score each time, thus demonstrating their increased word knowledge.

Picture This!

Skill: Identifying words using picture clues

Number of Players: Teams of 5 players

Object of the Game: To figure out vocabulary words from picture clues drawn by teammates

Materials

* game cards (page 29)
* drawing and writing materials
* timer

Getting Ready

Photocopy and cut apart a set of game cards (with or without the definitions).

How to Play

1. Divide the group into teams of five players.

2. Explain that this game is similar to charades, but instead of acting out the word, players will draw pictures to illustrate the word. Each team will have two minutes to guess the word from the pictures drawn by their teammate. When a teammate thinks he or she knows the word, that person writes the word. Players continue writing down their guesses until the word is identified.

3. Have the first "artist" on each team come to the front of the room, and show each the first word card to illustrate. When all artists have read the word, have them return to their teams. Then set the timer for two minutes and say "Go."

4. At the end of two minutes, the first team to correctly identify the word scores 5 points.

5. The next set of artists, the players who identified the word or the next player seated clockwise, come up to the front of the room to read the next card and prepare to draw the new word for their teammates to guess. Set the timer for the next round of play and say "Go."

6. The team with the highest score after each player has had a turn to draw wins.

More Ways to Play

* **Spelling Counts:** Play that the team to correctly guess the word gets 5 points if the word is spelled correctly, 3 if not. Or score 5 for correctly identifying the word, and add a bonus point if spelling is also correct.

* **Tricky Picture This:** Use compound words such as: *earthquake, library card, fire drill, tennis court, diving board, electric guitar, roof garden, living room, doubleheader,* and *merry-go-round.* **Note:** You may want to preteach different forms of compound words, including closed (*earthquake*), hyphenated (*merry-go-round*), and open (*living room*).

| escape | To break free, get loose, or leak out. |

| factory | A building where things are made in large numbers, often using machines. |

| freezing | Making or becoming very cold. |

| handsome | Nice-looking. |

| library | A place where books, magazines, newspapers, and videos are kept for reading or borrowing. |

As You Like It

Skill: Understanding similes

Number of Players: Groups of 3

Object of the Game: To write interesting, descriptive, original similes

Materials

* game cards (pages 31–32)
* writing and drawing materials

Getting Ready

Photocopy and cut apart the word cards, making a set for each group of players. Set aside the definition cards for another game.

How to Play

1. Explain that a simile is a comparison using the words *like* or *as*. Many clichés are similes—for example, *cold as ice.* Tell students that a cliché is a phrase or word that does not have the same impact because it has been overused. Then give them a simile for *cold* that is not a cliché, such as *cold as a winter morning on Pluto.*

2. Divide the class into groups of three. Give each group a set of cards.

3. Have groups write interesting similes for three or more words.

4. Have groups share their similes. Let the class vote for the best in a variety of categories, such as most descriptive, most original, funniest, longest, and shortest.

5. Have players select their favorite simile to illustrate.

More Ways to Play

* **Groaners:** Brainstorm a list of clichés, such as *cold as ice, hard as a rock, old as the hills, mad as a wet hen, dark as night,* and *deep as the ocean.* Write them on the bottom of blank cards and distribute randomly. Have students illustrate the cliché. On the reverse side, have them write a simile with the same meaning that is not a cliché and illustrate it.

* **Simile Search:** During independent reading time, have students work individually or with partners to find similes in books they are reading. Let them mark the similes they find with sticky notes. At the end of the period, have students count the number of similes they found, write the total and their initials on another sticky note, and place the note on the book cover. Then collect the books and redistribute randomly. The second reader checks that each noted phrase is a simile.

beautiful

Very pleasant to look at or listen to.

clumsy

Careless and awkward in movement or behavior.

delicate

1. Very pleasant to the senses.

2. Finely made.

3. Sensitive.

difficult

Not easy.

frighten

To make someone suddenly afraid or scared.

happy

Feeling or showing pleasure or joy; glad or content.

lost

1. To no longer have something you once had.

2. To have been beaten or defeated in a game.

smart

Clever and quick-thinking; bright.

strange

1. Different from the usual; odd.

2. Not known, heard, or seen before; not familiar.

strong

1. Powerful or having great force.

2. Hard to break; firm.

Vocabulary-Building Card Games: Grade 3 © 2008 by Liane B. Onish, Scholastic Teaching Resources

Mail Call

Skill: Using word knowledge

Number of Players: Small groups or whole class

Object of the Game: To use clues to identify a vocabulary word

How to Play

1. Select the first player to receive the "mail."

2. Choose a game card. Pass it around so that all other players can read the word.

3. Place the card in the envelope and deliver it to the player.

4. Play as you would play 20 Questions. The player with the mail asks questions to try to identify the word. Each question the player asks must have only a yes or no answer—for example: "Is it a verb?" "Does it begin with a blend?" "Does it have more than two syllables?"

5. When the player is ready to guess the word, he or she opens the envelope. Choose a new student to receive the mail, and play again.

More Ways to Play

- **Subject Mail Call:** Select content area words to use for Mail Call. If you identify for players the subject area, such as science or social studies, reduce the number of allowed questions to ten.

- **Classroom Magazines:** If your class uses a weekly newsmagazine, select words from recent issues to use in the game.

Materials

- game cards (any)
- envelope

Getting Ready

Photocopy and cut apart a set of word cards, such as those for Compound Charades (page 24) and As You Like It (page 30). Have as many cards as there are players. Set aside the definition cards for other games.

Word Shark

Skill: Using base words, prefixes, and suffixes to build words

Number of Players: Groups of 2 to 4

Object of the Game: To use the adjacent word parts on the game board to build words

Materials

* game board (page 35)
* game cards (pages 36–37)
* blank game card templates (page 61)
* timer

Getting Ready

Photocopy and cut apart a game board and set of word cards for each group of players. Set aside the definition cards for other games. Write the following affixes on blank cards (one per card): *re-*, *un-*, *-ed*, *-er*, *-est*, *-ing*, *-less*, *-ly*, *-ness*, *-s*. Trim the game cards to fit on the game board.

Teaching Tip

Review the meaning of prefixes *re-* (again) and *un-* (not) and suffixes *-ed* (happened in the past), *-er* (one who, or more), *-est* (most), *-ing* (happening now), *-less* (without), *-ly* (like or characteristic of), *-ness* (state or condition of), and *-s* (plural).

How to Play

1. Players sit where they can easily see the game board.

2. Players mix up the cards and place one card in each box on the game board. Be sure there are both base words and affixes in the game. Set the timer for three minutes.

3. Play as you would play Boggle. When you say "Go," players list the words they can see on the game board, using the words and word parts going across and down. Words must touch each other along one side to be used together. Words can be made from letters that start across and then turn the corner going down. For example (see below): Players score points for *repack*, *repacked*, and *packed*, but not *unpacked*.

4. At the end of three minutes, players read their words aloud. If all players agree that the words are real words, players then figure out their scores. Players score 1 point for each letter in a word.

5. Collect the cards, reshuffle, and deal a second round. Play three rounds. The player with the highest combined score wins.

re-	pack	do
paint	-ed	cover
un-	-ly	-ing

Word	Score
repack	6
repacked	8
repaint	7
repainted	9
unpainted	9
covering	8

More Ways to Play

* **Word Shark Match:** Play Word Shark without the game board. Give students a set of index cards with the affixes *re-*, *un-*, *-est*, *-ness*, *-s*, *-ed*, and *-ing* and the words *clean*, *check*, *cover*, *do*, *fair*, *fold*, *kind*, *pack*, *paint*, and *view*. Have them match affixes to base words. Students can use the affix cards as many times as needed to make as many words as possible. Students score 1 point for each letter in each word with a prefix and/or suffix.

* **Word Shark Attack:** Give pairs of students a page of a newspaper and highlighter pens. Have them find and highlight the words with affixes. Students score 1 point for each word with a suffix, 2 points for each word with a prefix, and 3 points for each word with both.

Word Shark

Vocabulary-Building Card Games: Grade 3

© 2008 by Liane B. Onish, Scholastic Teaching Resources

check

To look at something (often in order) to make sure that it is right.

clean

1. Not dirty or messy.

2. To remove dirt from something.

cover

1. To put one thing over another.

2. To teach or study thoroughly.

do

1. To perform or act.

2. To complete.

fair

1. Reasonable; just.

2. Neither good nor bad.

3. Clear and sunny weather.

Vocabulary-Building Card Games: Grade 3 © 2008 by Liane B. Onish, Scholastic Teaching Resources

fold

To bend over on itself.

kind

1. Friendly, helpful, and generous.

2. A group of the same or similar things.

pack

1. To put objects into a container.

2. A group of animals, people, or things.

3. A bag for carrying things on the back.

paint

1. A liquid to color or cover surfaces.

2. To make a picture or cover a surface.

view

1. The act of looking or seeing; sight.

2. What you can see from a certain place.

Vocabulary-Building Card Games: Grade 3 © 2008 by Liane B. Onish, Scholastic Teaching Resources

Hidden Homophones

Skill: Recognizing that certain words that sound the same have different spellings

Number of Players: Any

Object of the Game: To identify words from their definitions and then locate the words and their homophones in the puzzle

Materials

✳ Hidden Homophones puzzle (page 39)

✳ game cards (pages 40–43)

Getting Ready

Photocopy a puzzle for each player. Photocopy and cut apart the game cards (words and definitions). Each player will need a set of definition cards. Set aside the word cards for other games.

Homophone Pairs

been	bin
blew	blue
buy	by
one	won
right	write
sea	see
their	there
too	two
which	witch
wood	would

Answers: threw; through; in one side and out the other

How to Play

1. Players look at their definition cards, and then write the corresponding words and their homophones on the lines below the puzzle.

2. Players find and circle the listed words in the puzzle, scoring 5 points for each word they locate.

3. Players use the extra letters in the puzzle to spell the answer to the bonus question, and then write the meaning of the word. For correctly answering the bonus question, players add 5 extra points.

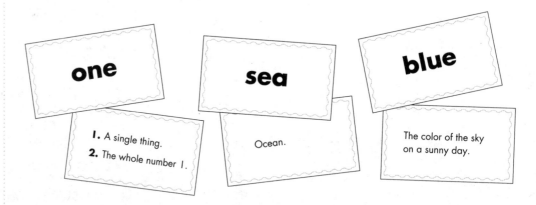

More Ways to Play

✳ **Hidden Words:** Make your own word searches using a blank grid and other definitions, synonyms, or antonyms.

✳ **Word Search Time:** After players list the words that match the definition cards, time how long it takes them to find all the words in the puzzle.

Hidden Homophones

Look at your definition cards. Write the words that go with the definitions on the lines below. Record homophones next to each other. Circle the words in the puzzle. Words can go across, down, and backward.

s	t	b	y	w	o	u	l	d
e	r	i	g	h	t	w	o	b
a	t	n	h	i	o	n	e	l
w	o	o	d	c	b	u	y	u
i	o	r	t	h	e	r	e	e
t	w	r	i	t	e	o	u	e
c	b	l	e	w	n	g	h	s
h	w	o	n	t	h	e	i	r

Homophone Pairs

1 _____   _____
2 _____   _____
3 _____   _____
4 _____   _____
5 _____   _____
6 _____   _____
7 _____   _____
8 _____   _____
9 _____   _____
10 _____   _____

Bonus

The remaining letters are a homophone for a word that means *the past tense of throw.*

The word is _____ . Its homophone is _____

and means _____

been

Was.

bin

A large covered container
or box for storing things.

blew

Made air come out through
your mouth.

blue

The color of the sky
on a sunny day.

buy

To get something by paying
money for it.

Vocabulary-Building Card Games: Grade 3 © 2008 by Liane B. Onish, Scholastic Teaching Resources

by

1. Next to, or beside.

2. Through the work of.

one

1. A single thing.

2. The whole number 1.

right

1. The side opposite left.

2. Correct; good, fair, and acceptable.

sea

Ocean.

see

1. To look at, find out, or discover; to understand.

2. To visit and spend time with.

their

Belonging to or having to do with them.

there

To, in, or at that place.

too

1. Very.

2. Also.

two

The whole number 2.

which

1. What one or ones.

2. The one or ones that.

Vocabulary-Building Card Games: Grade 3 © 2008 by Liane B. Onish, Scholastic Teaching Resources

witch

A person, especially a woman, believed to have magic powers.

won

Came in first in a contest.

wood

The hard substance that forms the trunk and branches of a tree.

would

1. Past tense of the helping verb *will*.

2. To request in a polite way.

write

1. To put down letters, words, or numbers on a surface.

2. To author or compose; to send a letter, message, or word of some kind.

Vocabulary-Building Card Games: Grade 3 © 2008 by Liane B. Onish, Scholastic Teaching Resources

Sentence-Ology

Skill: Using vocabulary words in sentences

Number of Players: 4

Object of the Game: To create sentences using vocabulary words

Materials

* scorecard (page 45)
* game cards (any)
* die or spinner with numerals 1–6
* dictionary

Getting Ready

Photocopy a scorecard for each player. Photocopy and cut apart any 30 word cards and their corresponding definition cards, such as those from Hidden Homophones (page 38).

How to Play

1. Mix up the word cards and place them in a pile. Set aside the definition cards for later use with this game. One player acts as dealer.

2. Each player (including the dealer) rolls the die. The dealer gives the player the same number of cards as shown on the die. If a player rolls a 1, he or she rolls again.

3. Players write one sentence in box 1 of their scorecard, using all the words from their game cards in the sentence. If all words can't be or are not used, the sentence will have a lower score.

4. When all players are finished writing their sentence, the first player reads his or her sentence aloud. If the other players agree that the sentence makes sense, and that all vocabulary words have been used correctly, the player scores the sentence (using the guidelines on the scorecard). All players read and score their sentences.

5. If a player challenges the sense of a sentence, or the use of a word, the group discusses the challenge. The dealer finds the definition card or looks up the word in the dictionary. If the sentence is successfully challenged, it is disqualified and the player must replace it with a new sentence. The challenger receives 5 bonus points.

6. Continue play until everyone has been the dealer (four rounds). Players total their points. High score wins.

More Ways to Play

* **60-Second Sentences:** Deal five cards to each of four players. The players set a timer for 60 seconds and then begin trading cards, all calling out at once the number of cards they wish to trade—for example, "one, one, one," or "three, three, three." When another player agrees to trade the same number of cards, the players make the trade without looking at one another's cards first. Players can trade as many times and with as many players as they wish, maintaining five cards in their hand at all times. At the end of 60 seconds, players have to make one sentence with the cards in their hand.

Name _____

Date _____

Sentence-Ology Scorecard

Sentences	Number of Words	Word Cards Used	3+ Syllables
1			
2			
3			
4			
Subtotals			
Grand Total			

Vocabulary-Building Card Games: Grade 3 © 2008 by Liane B. Onish, Scholastic Teaching Resources

Voca-Bees

Skill: Using vocabulary words in sentences

Number of Players: Whole class or large group

Object of the Game: To win words by correctly spelling, defining, and using the words in sentences

Materials

* Bee Cards (page 61)
* paper clips

Getting Ready

Photocopy enough blank Bee Cards so each player will have a turn. On each pair of cards, write a word on one side and the definition on the other. Fold in half and paper-clip closed if desired.

How to Play

1. Mix up the cards and place them in a pile, word-side up.

2. Divide the group into two teams. Have teams line up on opposite sides of the room.

3. Read the top word for team 1. The first player for team 1 repeats the word, spells it, tells what it means, and uses it in a sentence. If the player is correct, the player gets the Bee Card. If the player is incorrect, a player from the other team can answer.

4. Read the next word for the first player on team 2.

5. Continue as above until all players on both teams have played. The team that has collected the most cards at the end of the game wins.

More Ways to Play

* **Define-a-Bee:** Read the definition, not the word. Players identify and spell the word that goes with the definition.

* **Beat the Buzzer:** Have players pair up and set a timer for a minute. How many words can they complete (read the word and give the definition, or read the definition and identify the word) before the buzzer?

Cloze Call

Skill: Using knowledge of word categories and context clues

Number of Players: 2 or more teams

Object of the Game: To use knowledge of categories and context clues to complete cloze sentences

How to Play

1. Write each category name on a whiteboard. Divide the group into two or more teams.

2. The first team chooses a category. Select a card at random from the corresponding envelope of clues and read it aloud. Repeat if necessary.

3. To answer, players repeat the cloze sentence with the answer in the blank, and then repeat the answer word. The team scores 5 points for a correct answer. Then the next player on the team takes a turn. The second player may stay with the same category or select a new one. The team continues to play until they miss a word.

4. Repeat steps 2 and 3 for each additional team.

5. When all the cards in a category have been used, the category is closed. Play until all clue cards have been selected or a designated amount of time is up. The team with the highest score wins.

More Ways to Play

❋ **Spelling Counts:** Players may score an additional two points for their team by correctly spelling the answer.

❋ **Ding!** Assign each team a different "buzzer" sound (for example, "bzzzzzzz" and "ding"). Choose a team to go first (or let teams roll a die and give the first turn to the highest roller). This team selects the category. Take a card at random from the corresponding envelope and read the clue aloud. All teams then try to be the first to figure out the missing word. The first team to sound its buzzer tells what word is missing. Have this team repeat the sentence with the missing word filled in. The team scores 5 points for a correct answer. If the answer is incorrect, remaining teams may attempt to answer. The team to answer correctly chooses the next category, and play continues.

Materials

❋ category chart and clue cards (page 48)

❋ dictionaries

❋ envelopes

Getting Ready

Photocopy and cut apart the clue cards. To play with all words from each of the ten sample categories, you'll need 49 clue cards. Have students work in small groups to complete the cards, copying the category for each word, writing a cloze sentence with a blank space for the target word, and filling in the answer. Place each set of clue cards in an envelope labeled with the category name.

Category Chart

Category	Description	Sample Words
Dis- Is It! (Prefixes)	Words that begin with the prefix *dis-*	discontinue, discount, displease, disrespect, distrust
Same/Difference	Synonyms or antonyms	happy, healthy, loud, mild, smart
A Is for . . .	Words that begin with the letter *a*	acrobat, approach, arrange, asleep, awful
The Power of Three Syllables	Three-syllable words	allergic, capital, dinosaur, interview, messenger
Size It Up	Size words	enormous, huge, mammoth, minute, towering
Wear It	Clothing words	goggles, kimono, shawl, suspenders, vest
Worldly Words	Geography words	canyon, island, peninsula, stream, valley
Properly	Proper nouns	Abraham Lincoln, Caribbean Sea, Grand Canyon, Hawaii, Statue of Liberty
Multiple Sports	Words that have sports and nonsports meanings (use two clues for each word: one for the sports definition and one for general meaning)	dribble, field, goal, slide, steal
Sensitivity	Words that appeal to the senses	fragile, juicy, scratchy, soothing, spicy

Cloze Call Clue Card

Category: _____

Clue: _____

_____

Answer: _____

Cloze Call Clue Card

Category: _____

Clue: _____

_____

Answer: _____

Vocabulary-Building Card Games: Grade 3 © 2008 by Liane B. Onish, Scholastic Teaching Resources

What's in a Word?

Skill: Recognizing features of words

Number of Players: Teams of 2 to 3 players

Object of the Game: To make new words using the letters of multisyllabic words

How to Play

1. Divide the class into teams of two to three players each. Place the same multisyllabic word card facedown in front of each team.

2. Set the timer for three minutes. When you say "Go!" players use the letters of their word to make short words. Decide in advance if proper nouns are allowed.

3. At the end of three minutes, have teams compare lists. Teams get 1 point for each word. Alternate scoring system: Teams score 1 point for each word that no other team has.

4. Repeat for other vocabulary words.

More Ways to Play

❋ **Move Those Letters:** Provide letter tiles to match the letters in each word so that students can manipulate them to make new words.

❋ **Score More:** Encourage attention to word parts with this scoring variation: Players on a team multiply the number of words they made that no other team made by the number of syllables in the word. For example, if a team made three words from the letters in *beautiful* that no other team made, the score would be 9 points (3 x 3).

Materials

❋ game cards (any multisyllabic words)

❋ blank game card templates (page 61; optional)

❋ writing materials

❋ timer

Getting Ready

Photocopy and cut apart any number of multisyllabic word cards. Make duplicate sets, one for each team. You will need a different word for each round of play. To use words not included in this book, photocopy and cut apart blank game card templates, and write desired multisyllabic words on them (one per card).

Vocabulary Baseball

Skill: Identifying vocabulary words by definition

Number of Players: 2 teams

Object of the Game: To run the bases and score by identifying vocabulary words

Materials

* game cards (any)
* glue

Getting Ready

Photocopy and cut apart any word and definition cards, such as those from As You Like It (page 30) and Hidden Homophones (page 38). Cut apart the cards in such a way as to keep each word and definition pair intact. Fold at the center, and glue back to back to create flash cards.

How to Play

1. Divide the class into two teams. Designate corners of the room as follows: home, first, second, and third bases. The pitcher (teacher or student) sits in the middle of the room.

2. The team "at bat" lines up along the side of the room by home base. The first player moves to home base and the pitcher reads the first definition. If the batter correctly identifies the word (with the pitcher checking the back of the card to confirm), he or she goes to first base.

3. Continue reading definitions to new batters. Players move from base to base as batters correctly identify vocabulary words. Players returning to home plate score 1 point each for their team.

4. Each incorrect answer is an "out." When the team at bat has three outs, the second team is up. Play each game for four or more innings.

More Ways to Play

* **And the Meaning Is…:** Instead of reading definitions, read vocabulary words and have batters supply the definitions.

* **Single, Double, Triple:** Let players decide together which vocabulary words are worth (based on difficulty) a single, double, or triple base "hit." Color-code the words accordingly (or place them in three separate piles). Batters choose their base, and the pitcher then reads the definition of a word at that difficulty level. Batters who correctly identify the word move to that base (first, second, or third), and play continues as above.

Sorting Hats

Skill: Identifying parts of speech

Number of Players: 1 or 2 players, or 2 teams

Object of the Game: To sort word cards by parts of speech

How to Play

One or Two Players:

1. Organize the definition cards by the parts of speech the matching words represent. Place each set of cards facedown in the correct hats.

2. Review parts of speech: nouns, verbs, adjectives, and adverbs.

3. Mix up a set of word cards for each player. Place the three hats nearby.

4. Set the timer for one minute. Players sort the words by parts of speech.

5. At the end of one minute, players count the number of cards in the correct hats by matching their word cards to the definition cards in the hat.

Teams:

1. Review parts of speech: nouns, verbs, adjectives, and adverbs.

2. Place the three hats on a table at the front of the room. Sort definition cards according to the parts of speech their matching words represent. Place the definition cards facedown in the correct hats.

3. Mix up each set of word cards, and place them facedown in front of each team. Have teams line up at the back of the room.

4. The first player on each team takes the top card, runs to the front of the room, and places the card in the correct hat. Then the player runs to the back of the line. The game continues with each player in turn placing a word card in the correct hat.

5. The team matches word cards to definition cards to confirm words are correctly sorted. The first team to accurately sort all their cards wins.

More Ways to Play

❋ **A Second Sort:** Have players further sort the words in each hat. For example, they can sort nouns by people, places, and things.

❋ **Her Sorting Hats:** Focus the game on nouns, pronouns, possessive pronouns, and proper nouns. Make a separate hat for each category.

Materials

❋ three hats
❋ sticky notes
❋ game cards (any)
❋ index cards
❋ glue
❋ timer

Getting Ready

Use sticky notes to label the hats as follows: "Nouns," "Verbs," "Adjectives and Adverbs." Photocopy and cut apart any word cards from the book as follows: 10 nouns, 10 verbs, and 20 adjectives and adverbs (combined). For one player only, make one set of word cards. For two players or two teams, make two sets of word cards and glue each set to different-color index cards. Photocopy and cut apart matching definition cards (40 total).

Opposites Attract

Skill: Recognizing antonyms

Number of Players: An even number of players

Object of the Game: To identify antonyms

Materials

❋ game cards (pages 53–60)

Getting Ready

Photocopy and cut apart the game cards. Use only the word cards for this game. Set aside the definition cards for other games. Each player will need one word card.

How to Play

1. Review what antonyms are: words that have the opposite meaning. Invite students to suggest antonyms they know.

2. Mix up the cards. Distribute randomly one card facedown to each player. Tell students not to look at their cards until you say "Go."

3. Say "Go," and have players find the player who has an antonym for their word. When players pair up, have them sit down and discuss the meaning of their words.

More Ways to Play

❋ **A. T. M. (Antonym Time Match):** Use a timer to see how long it takes the class to pair up all the antonyms.

❋ **Synonym Siblings:** Play with synonym pairs: *begin-start, appear-look, arrive-reach, anger-rage, below-under, call-yell, divide-split, during-while, end-finish, fix-mend, giant-huge, grow-develop, messy-sloppy, quick-fast, revise-change, pick-choose, uproar-noise, understand-know, wash-clean, well-healthy.*

above

1. Higher up than, or over.

2. More than.

add

1. To find the sum.

2. To put one thing with another.

all

Everything.

answer

The solution to a problem.

asleep

Sleeping.

awake

Not sleeping.

back

The opposite end or side from the front.

begin

To start.

below

Lower than.

blame

To say or think that someone or something is at fault.

Vocabulary-Building Card Games: Grade 3 © 2008 by Liane B. Onish, Scholastic Teaching Resources

break

To separate into pieces.

cry

1. To weep tears.
2. To shout out.

different

Not the same.

dislike

1. To not like.
2. To be opposed to.

earn

To receive payment for work done.

Vocabulary-Building Card Games: Grade 3 © 2008 by Liane B. Onish, Scholastic Teaching Resources

end

1. The last part of something.
2. To finish.

enjoy

To get pleasure from.

evening

The time of day between the late afternoon and the early part of the night.

false

Not true or correct; not real.

forgive

To pardon someone, or to stop blaming the person for something.

Vocabulary-Building Card Games: Grade 3 © 2008 by Liane B. Onish, Scholastic Teaching Resources

front

The part that faces forward.

get

1. To obtain.

2. To become.

give

To hand to another person.

hear

To listen to.

heavy

Weighing a lot.

Vocabulary-Building Card Games: Grade 3 © 2008 by Liane B. Onish, Scholastic Teaching Resources

ignore

To take no notice of.

laugh

To make sounds with the voice that show amusement.

light

1. Brightness, as from the sun or a lamp.

2. To start something burning.

3. Weighing a little.

morning

The time of day between midnight and noon or sunrise and noon.

none

1. No one or not one; not any or no part.

2. Not at all.

Vocabulary-Building Card Games: Grade 3 © 2008 by Liane B. Onish, Scholastic Teaching Resources

Vocabulary-Building Card Games: Grade 3 © 2008 by Liane B. Onish, Scholastic Teaching Resources

question

1. A sentence that asks.

2. A problem or doubt.

repair

To make something work again, or to put back together something that is broken.

same

1. Exactly alike in every way.

2. Not changed or different.

shout

To call out loudly.

spend

1. To use money to buy things.

2. To pass time.

subtract

To take one number away from another.

tame

1. Taken from a wild state and trained.

2. Gentle or not afraid; not shy.

true

1. Agreeing with the facts; not false.

2. Real or genuine.

whisper

To talk very quietly or softly.

wild

1. Not tame; out of control.

2. An area in its natural state; wilderness.

Vocabulary-Building Card Games: Grade 3 © 2008 by Liane B. Onish, Scholastic Teaching Resources

Wild
Card

Wild
Card

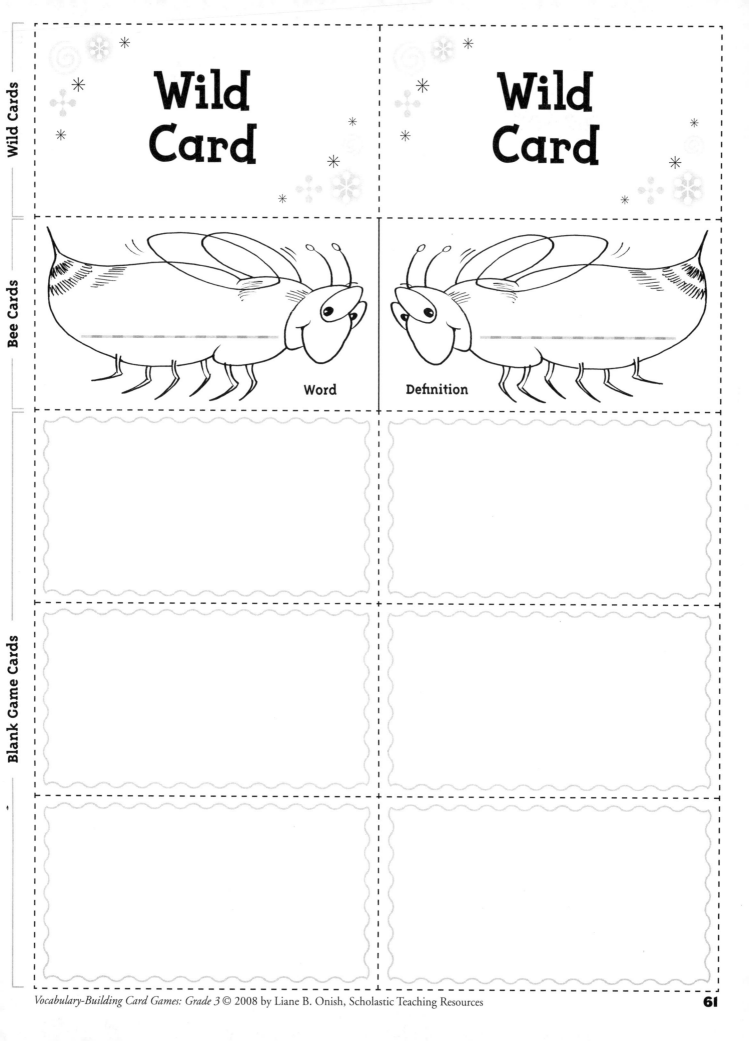

Word

Definition

absent	Not present.
adventure	An exciting or dangerous experience.
again	One more time.
always	At all times; every time.
around	1. Surrounding. 2. More or less.

Vocabulary-Building Card Games: Grade 3 © 2008 by Liane B. Onish, Scholastic Teaching Resources

astronaut

Someone who travels in space.

away

1. Moving from.

2. Distant from a place.

3. Not at home.

because

For the reason that; since.

behind

On the other side; toward the back.

believe

1. To feel sure that something is true.

2. To support someone or something.

bring

To take someone or something with you.

call

1. To name.

2. To shout out.

3. To telephone.

carry

To hold on to something and take it somewhere.

city

A very large or important town.

complete

1. Having all the parts that are needed or wanted.

2. In every way.

3. To finish something.

Vocabulary-Building Card Games: Grade 3 © 2008 by Liane B. Onish, Scholastic Teaching Resources

could

1. Was able to.

2. Was allowed to do something.

curtain

A piece of fabric pulled across a stage or window to cover it.

daughter

Someone's female child.

does

The present tense of *do* used with *he*, *she*, *it*, or singular nouns.

done

1. A past form of *do*.

2. Cooked long enough.

draw

1. To make a picture.

2. To pull something.

3. Competition ending in a tie.

during

Within a certain time.

easily

An act that does not need much effort, ability, or training.

either

One or the other of two.

enough

As much as is needed or wanted.

Vocabulary-Building Card Games: Grade 3 © 2008 by Liane B. Onish, Scholastic Teaching Resources

example

1. Something typical of a larger group.
2. A model to follow.
3. A question or problem given with its answer.

fantasy

1. Something you imagine that is not likely to happen in real life.
2. A story with strange or magical elements.

far

1. A great distance.
2. Very much.

flavor

A taste.

fly

1. To travel through the air.
2. To move or pass quickly.
3. An insect with two wings.
4. A flap on pants covering a zipper or buttons.

follow

1. To be guided by someone or something.
2. To go behind someone.
3. To come after.
4. To obey.

fortune

1. Chance or good luck.
2. A large amount of money.

found

1. To set up or start, such as a school.
2. Past tense of *find*.
3. To discover or come across.
4. A valuable or important discovery.

full

1. Holding as much as possible.
2. Whole, complete.
3. Having a large number of something.

going

The act of moving away from or toward a place.

Vocabulary-Building Card Games: Grade 3 © 2008 by Liane B. Onish, Scholastic Teaching Resources

Vocabulary-Building Card Games: Grade 3 © 2008 by Liane B. Onish, Scholastic Teaching Resources

group

1. A number of things that go together or are alike in some way.
2. A number of people who gather together.

grow

1. To increase in size, length, or amount.
2. To become.
3. To plant something and look after it.

held

To have carried, supported, or kept.

idea

A thought, a plan, or an opinion.

its

Related to or belonging to something.

it's

A short form of *it is* or *it has*.

just

1. Exactly.
2. A very short time ago.
3. Barely.
4. Nothing more than.
5. What is fair and right.

knew

To already be familiar with a person, place, or piece of information.

learn

1. To gain knowledge or skill.
2. To memorize.
3. To discover news.

left

1. The side from which you begin to read English.
2. Past tense of *leave*.
3. To have abandoned.
4. The opposite of *right*.

Vocabulary-Building Card Games: Grade 3 © 2008 by Liane B. Onish, Scholastic Teaching Resources

live (liv)

1. Remain alive.
2. To have your home somewhere.

live (live)

1. Alive or living.
2. On TV as it happens.

may

1. Used to say something is possible or likely.
2. To ask or give permission.
3. To express hope or a wish.
4. The fifth month when capitalized.

measure

1. To find out the size or weight of something.
2. An amount.
3. A bar of music.

middle

The halfway point (between two points or in the center).

monitor

1. A student who has a special job to do in the classroom.
2. The computer screen.
3. To keep a check on something over time.

monster

1. A large, fierce, horrible creature.

2. A very evil or cruel person.

3. Huge. (adjective)

month

One of the 12 parts that make up a year.

much

1. Great in amount or degree.

2. Very.

music

A pleasant arrangement of sounds, such as in a song.

must

1. To have to.

2. To be forced or required.

Vocabulary-Building Card Games: Grade 3 © 2008 by Liane B. Onish, Scholastic Teaching Resources

Vocabulary-Building Card Games: Grade 3 © 2008 by Liane B. Onish, Scholastic Teaching Resources

neither

Not either. Used with *nor* to show two negative choices.

never

At no time or not ever; not at all.

once

1. One time.
2. In the past.

plenty

A large number or amount that is more than enough.

problem

1. A difficult situation that needs to be figured out or overcome.
2. A puzzle or question to be solved.

pull

1. To move forward or toward.
2. To tug or pluck.
3. To stretch or strain a part of the body.

put

1. To play, lay, or move something.
2. To express in words.
3. An athletic event.

ready

1. Prepared.
2. Willing.
3. Likely or about to do.
4. Quick.

remain

1. To stay in the same place.
2. To be left behind or left over.

round

1. Shaped like a circle or a ball.
2. A series of repeated actions or events.
3. A complete game.
4. To make or become circular; to go around.

Vocabulary-Building Card Games: Grade 3 © 2008 by Liane B. Onish, Scholastic Teaching Resources

seize

1. To grab or take hold of suddenly.
2. To arrest or capture.

shall

Used with other verbs to show future time or action that is needed, or to ask a question or offer an idea.

should

Used with other verbs to show a duty or something that is likely, expected, or that might happen.

simply

1. In a simple way; plainly.
2. Merely or just.
3. Completely; very (as modifier: The puppy is simply adorable).

sometimes

At a time that is not stated or known.

Vocabulary-Building Card Games: Grade 3 © 2008 by Liane B. Onish, Scholastic Teaching Resources

start

1. To begin to move, act, or happen.

2. To jump in surprise.

straight

1. Not bent.

2. Level or even.

3. Honest; correct.

4. Immediately or directly.

sure

1. Having no doubt.

2. Certain to happen, impossible to avoid.

3. Firm or steady.

talk

1. To speak.

2. A conversation or speech.

target

1. Something that is aimed or shot at.

2. A goal or aim.

Vocabulary-Building Card Games: Grade 3 © 2008 by Liane B. Onish, Scholastic Teaching Resources

Vocabulary-Building Card Games: Grade 3 © 2008 by Liane B. Onish, Scholastic Teaching Resources

these

The plural of *this*.

those

The plural of *that*.

though

1. In spite of the fact that; although; yet; but.

2. However; nevertheless.

thought

1. An idea or opinion.

2. The act of thinking.

through

1. In one side and out the other.

2. From the beginning to the end.

3. Finished.

together

1. With one another.

2. Into one group or place.

3. At the same time.

trouble

1. A difficult, dangerous, or upsetting state.

2. To worry, annoy, or disturb.

3. To ask for help.

upon

On.

usual

Normal, common, or expected.

vacant

Empty or not occupied.

Vocabulary-Building Card Games: Grade 3 © 2008 by Liane B. Onish, Scholastic Teaching Resources

village

A small group of houses that make up a community.

walk

1. To move along on foot.

2. A journey on foot.

warm

1. A bit hot; not cold.

2. Holding in body heat.

3. Very friendly.

4. To increase the temperature.

while

1. A period of time.

2. During the time that.

3. Although.

word

1. A unit of sounds or letters that has meaning.

2. Short conversation.

3. News or message.

worth

1. Have a value in money.

2. Deserving, or good enough.

year

A period of 365 days divided into 12 months.

yesterday

1. The day before today.

2. The recent past.

young

1. Someone or something that has or had lived for a short time.

2. The offspring of an animal.

zone

A separate area used for a special purpose.

Vocabulary-Building Card Card Games: Grade 3 © 2008 by Liane B. Onish, Scholastic Teaching Resources